The Art of Spoken Word Poetry

(Special Edition)

BY DARRELL MITCHELL II

Helpful tools, tips, and techniques that can improve your spoken word poetry performance.

Table of contents

Introduction

The goal of this book is to provide a "How to" guide with principles that can be used to improve content and stage performance. This book doesn't come with the promise of making you a great spoken word artist or the experience of a world-famous poet. Instead, it provides tools, examples of techniques and it offers tips, which if practiced correctly, can improve your confidence, focus and execution. Every artist comes equipped with their own amount of creativity, imagination, and inspiration. Storytelling is a big part of spoken word poetry as well, but if you are not able to tell that story or relay a message clearly to people then there might as well be no one listening.

By utilizing examples from the P-Arts (Performing Arts) program and workshop courses that have been implemented in the San Fernando Valley, Los Angeles, and San Diego area of Southern California through DM Ink Publishing. You will be able to apply the same techniques which have helped many spoken word artist and poets to develop and improve their skill. I've spent years performing, writing, reading, listening, and publishing spoken word poetry and it has been a great learning experience. As a fan, an artist and facilitator of workshops I can relate to the frustration of having a good performance piece and not being able to get the message through to the audience. Or being nervous and not having any prior training or years of experience that would assist with speaking in a small or large venue. By incorporating a few tips used by spoken word poet professionals, readers will find this book will:

-Provide helpful tips of structuring the content to your piece so that it flows.

-Go over various spoken word techniques.

-Provide tools to improve your delivery.

The areas of focus covered are just a few pieces to a larger puzzle in the areas of communication and writing that could benefit an aspiring spoken word artist.

This book has been used in performing arts workshops and the tools have been successfully applied during performances and network writing sessions. Principles are universal and I'm not saying that every artist needs to adapt these tips in order to be considered great, because in the spoken word poetry market everyone is unique, or at least they should be. Each person has a story to tell, and it can have a powerful effect depending on how the writer delivers it.

Many times, well written poems are mumbled when spoken, or they are recited but not fueled by the passion needed to powerfully express the message or content. There are certain tools listed in this book that can assist in making sure that the message is not lost during the performance process. Once again these are just helpful items that will assist with making sure if anything else your message is delivered clearly, the rest is up to you.

Practice makes perfect and by incorporating beneficial techniques into your performance it will strengthen those areas which you would like improve in. Being a writer the topics we write about often change as well as what is relevant and trending. Principles will never change; they are only tools that help us sharpen our skills which will allow us to be the best that we can be. The sky is the limit, so I hope this book helps artist and writers reach their full potential and open doors to new opportunities.

Spoken Word

Spoken word is often used to describe works or performances that consist of mostly one person singing or speaking. Rules are often thrown out the window when it comes to this art form but, whether you're speaking naturally or singing musically this often can be found to be a clearly different format and separate from rapping. Rhythm and melody have been incorporated into the art form, but spoken word is more known for narration or speaking as the person would in conversation. In entertainment circles, spoken word performances generally consist of storytelling and or poetry either with or without rhyme.

When you take a look at historical Hebrew poetry for example, you'll notice that it contains almost no rhyme. But the poems were written over a portion of time of at least a thousand years. Over that length of time, the pronunciation of words in any language can change. Words that rhymed at the beginning of that period may no longer rhyme at the end of that period. In addition to that different tribal groups or other groups of speakers certainly pronounced words differently in one and the same era. You can even hear some artist rhyme "again" with "pain" while others rhyme "again" with "pen" in today's music and spoken word.

Performance poetry

Performance poetry is poetry that is specifically arranged for or during performance before an audience. The term was once popular when describing poetry that was written or composed for performance rather than print distribution.

Spoken word can be used to inform or make people conscious of some aspect pertaining to life also. Spoken word poetry, has allowed people to share and express their views, emotions, life experiences or information. The views of spoken word artists can cover not only spirituality, political powers, and love but any other aspect of life as well. This is what can give a piece that emotional power but, at the same time, a lack of emotion can set a poem apart from others. It depends on the topic, and life experiences are highly favored, especially when the person has actually lived through the experience.

ShadoWork, for instance, is a term that describes cooperative stage work using poetry and movement. By combining (simple) theatrical movement with the full range of voice and stage in ways designed to draw deeper attention to the text. To go even further, now you have writers extending spoken word to short prose productions and fusing performance poetry with dance.

Metaphor

A **metaphor** is a comparison between two things that are similar in some way, often used to help explain something or make it easier to understand. It's also a likeness between two objects or ideas which is expressed by the use of a metaphorical word in place of some other word. For example: "Her smile was like sparkling diamonds". *Metaphor* also relates to symbolic figures of speech that use association, comparison, or resemblance to achieve their effects. The word *metaphor* in Latin *means* "carrying over", and in the Greek it means to "transfer", from.

A parable is like a metaphor that has been extended to form a brief, clear and reasonable fictional story. Biblical parables have been considered as extended metaphors.

A parable is a short tale that illustrates universal truth, one of the simplest of narratives. It sketches a setting, describes an action, and shows the results. It often involves a character facing a moral dilemma or making a questionable decision and then suffering the consequences from choice. As with a fable, a parable generally relates a single, simple, consistent action, without unrelated detail or distracting conditions.

The word "parable" comes from the Greek ", the name was given by skilled Greek writers to any imaginative illustration in the form of a brief story. Later it came to mean a made-up narrative, generally referring to something that might naturally occur, by which spiritual and moral matters might be communicated.

A parable's parallel meaning is unspoken and understood, though not ordinarily secret. The defining characteristic of the parable is the presence of a strongly held belief suggesting how a person should behave or believe. Aside from providing guidance and suggestions for proper action in life, parables frequently use metaphorical language which allows people to more easily discuss difficult or complex ideas.

In common modern uses of "parables," though their meaning is never plainly stated, parables are not generally held to be hidden or secret but on the other hand are typically straightforward and obvious. It is the symbolic expression of meaning in the story that typically features hidden meanings.

Parables are favored in the expression of spiritual concepts. The best-known sources of parables are located in the *Bible*, which contains many parables in the Gospels section of the New Testament.

Biblical parables are outwardly simple and memorable stories, often with imagery, and each conveys a message. Although these parables seem simple, the messages they convey are deep, and central to the teachings of Jesus. These parables are also internal comparisons where nature is used as a witness for the spiritual world.

In Western civilization, these parables formed the prototype for the term *parable* and in the modern age, even among those who know little of the Bible, the parables of Jesus remain some of the best-known stories around the globe.

As a translation of the Hebrew word *mashal*, the word parable can also refer to a riddle. In all times in their history the Jews were familiar with teaching by means of parables and a number of parables also exist in the Old Testament of the bible. That's why the use of parables by Jesus was considered a natural teaching method that fit into the tradition of his time. They have been quoted, taught, and discussed since the very beginnings of Christianity.

Inspiration

The word *"inspiration"* comes from the Latin noun *"inspiratio"* and from the verb *"inspirare"*. *"Inspirare"* is a multipart term resulting from the Latin prefix *"in"* (inside, into) and the verb *"spirare"* (to breathe). *"Inspirare"* meant originally *"to blow into"*. It also was known to mean "to breathe deeply" and assumed also the figurative sense of "to instill [something] in the heart or in the mind of someone".

Thought inspiration is a form of divine inspiration in which revelation takes place in the mind of the writer, as opposed to verbal inspiration, in which the word of God is communicated directly to the writer.

Inspiration refers to an unconscious burst of creativity in a literary, musical, or other artistic ventures such as rapping. Literally, the word means "breathed upon,". Inspiration is also a divine matter in Hebrew poetics.

Inspiration comes into play before consciousness and outside of skill. Technique and performance are independent of inspiration, and therefore it is possible for the non-spoken word poet to be inspired and for a poet or to be lacking to the inspiration. In Hebrew poetics, inspiration is similarly a divine matter. However, inspiration is also a matter of revelation for the prophets, and the two concepts are intermixed to some degree. Revelation is a conscious process, where the writer or artist is aware and interactive with the vision, while inspiration is involuntary and received without any complete understanding.

Inspiration in the story is the product of grace: it is unsought (though desired), uncontrolled, and irresistible, and the poet's performance involves his whole mind and body, but it is basically a gift.

Inspiration was evidence of genius, and genius was a thing that the poet could take pride in, even though he could not claim to have created it himself.

In modern psychology, inspiration is not frequently studied, but it is generally seen as an entirely internal process. In each view, however, whether philosophical belief or mystical, inspiration is, by its nature, beyond control.

Creativity

Creativity is the ability to generate innovative ideas and manifest them from thought into reality. The process involves original thinking and then producing.

Creativity comes from the Latin term *creō* "to create, make". The ways in which societies have understood the concept of creativity have changed throughout history, as has the term itself. Originally in the Christian period: "*creatio*" came to designate God's act of *Ex nihilo*, "creation from nothing." "*Creatio*" thus had a different meaning than "*facere*" ("to make") and did not apply to human functions.
 For over a century and a half, during the renaissance era the idea of

human creativity met with resistance, due to the fact that the term "creation" was reserved for creation "from nothing."

Although neither the Greeks nor the Romans had a word that directly corresponded to the word "creativity," their art, architecture, music, inventions and discoveries provide numerous examples of what today would be described as creative works.

Creative thought

Creative thought is a mental process involving creative problem solving and the discovery of new ideas or concepts, or new associations of the existing ideas or concepts, fueled by the process of either conscious or unconscious insight..

Although naturally a simple phenomenon, it is in fact quite complex. It has been studied from the various professional perspectives. The studies have covered everyday creativity, exceptional creativity and even artificial creativity. Unlike many trends in science, there is no single, authoritative perspective or definition of creativity. And unlike many occurrences in psychology, there is no standardized measuring technique.

Creativity is typically used to refer to the act of producing new ideas, approaches or actions, while innovation is the process of both generating and applying such creative ideas in some specific situation.

Creativity leads to capital, and creative products are protected by intellectual property laws.

Creativity techniques are methods that promote original thoughts by facilitating different and/or joint thinking. Some techniques require groups of two or more people while other techniques can be accomplished alone. These methods include word games, written exercises and different types of creativeness used in the DM Ink Publishing spoken word workshops. Creativity techniques can be used to develop new materials for artistic purposes or to solve problems.

Improvisation is a creative process which can be spoken, written, or composed without previous research. Improvisation also called ad-libbing or referred to as winging it and free styling, can lead to the discovery of new ways to act, new patterns of thought and practices, or new structures. Improvisation is used in the creation of music, theatre, and other various forms. Many artists also use this technique to help their creative flow.

Randomness is considered the introduction of chance elements. The terms are commonly found in music, art, and literature, particularly in spoken word poetry. Other ways of practicing randomness include coin tossing, picking something out of a hat, or selecting random words from a dictionary.

Imagination, also called the faculty of **imagining**, is the ability of forming mental images, sensations, and concepts, in a moment when they are not perceived through sight, hearing or other senses. It is the work of the mind that helps create. Imagination helps provide meaning to experience and understanding to knowledge; it is a fundamental facility through which people make sense of real life, and it also plays a key role in the learning process. A basic training for imagination is listening to storytelling, performance poetry or spoken word, in which the accuracy of the chosen word or words is the underlying factor to "stir up imaginative worlds."

Imagination is the faculty through which we internally process everything. The things that we touch see and hear band together to form a "picture" via our imagination.

It is accepted as the natural ability and method of inventing partial or complete personal realms within the mind from elements resulting from sense perceptions of the world. The term is technically used in psychology for the process of stimulating in the mind, percepts of objects previously given in sense perception. Since this use of the term conflicts with that of ordinary language, some specialist have preferred to describe this process as "imaging" or "imagery" or to speak of it as "reproductive" as opposed to "productive" or "constructive" imagination. Imagined images are seen with the "mind's eye."

Imagination can also be expressed through stories such as fairy tales, fables, or fantasies. Throughout history some of the most famous inventions or entertainment products were created from the inspiration of someone's imagination. The common use of the term is for the process of forming new images in the mind that have not been previously experienced, or at least only partially or in different combinations.

Imagination is an experimental blank canvas of the mind used to create theories and ideas based on functions. Taking objects from real perceptions, the imagination uses complex IF-functions to create new or revised ideas. This part of the mind is vital to developing better and easier ways to accomplish old and new tasks. These experimental ideas can be safely conducted inside a mental virtual world and then, if the idea is probable and the function is true, the idea can be manifested in reality. Imagination is the key to new development of the mind and can be shared with others, progressing collectively as a group.

Imagination vs. Belief

Imagination differs fundamentally from belief because the person understands that what is personally invented by the mind does not necessarily impact the course of action taken in the real world while beliefs are part of what one holds as truths about both the shared and personal worlds. The play of imagination, apart from the obvious limitations is conditioned only by the general trend of the mind at a given moment. Belief, on the other hand, is immediately related to realistic activity: it is perfectly possible to imagine oneself a millionaire, but unless one believes it one does not act as if it is so. Belief tries hard to conform to the subject's experienced conditions or faith in the possibility of those circumstances, whereas imagination free.

Imagination, because of having freedom from external limitations, can often become a source of real pleasure and unnecessary suffering. The learned distinction between imagination and belief depends in practice on religion, tradition, and culture. Consistent with this idea, imagining pleasurable and fearful events is found to connect with emotional circuits involved in emotional perception and experience.

Message content structure

Moviemakers work hard to make their movies gripping from start to finish. It is not enough to like the subject of a movie or find it interesting in the beginning or enjoyable in parts. To be memorable, it has to capture your attention at the start and hold your attention throughout.

Highly successful movies do two things really well to engage the people in an audience and make them respond:
They tell stories, every movie tells a story, and the stories that work

best are simple ones. The story also needs drama and excitement to keep the audience fully involved.

They create characters - Great movie characters come alive. They have strong personalities. Also, the audience has to be able to identify with them.

If you want your performance to fully engage your audience members, you should create strong characters and tell a story that is easy to follow.

Inject excitement into the story - create a sense of anticipation. Make sure your performance has several peaks, or periods when the action you're describing is particularly intense and interesting.

Making characters interesting

In spoken word, you, the speaker, are the strongest character. It is your animation and energy that will make your story, and the characters in it, come alive for the audience. You should:

Create strong personalities—People need to be able to visualize the characters, give an example of something they said. You might also describe a place, a factory, or a special object.

Create characters people can identify with—the audience needs to know what people in your story are thinking and feeling in order to identify with them. Also, describe the atmosphere of places.

Your spoken word story or content is not trying to compete with a movie, but you need to know how to apply the basic techniques that enable the professionals to hold an audience by telling a story and creating characters.

Varying content and delivery style

Without variety, your performance piece has the potential to be boring. All successful performances contain different kinds of content and a variety of delivery styles.

Constant variety of content and delivery style means that audience interest and excitement is always maintained. People are eager to know what's coming next.

Varying delivery

With spoken word, you have to generate the variety yourself to make sure that your delivery does not become uninteresting or boring. Your performance needs to have high-energy periods. It also needs more relaxed, lower-energy periods. High-energy moments generate excitement. Lower-energy moments help the audience to reflect on something you've said.

There is more than one way to achieve a high-energy period in your performance. You can talk faster or a little louder. If you do either or both of these things, you will become more animated, and the overall impression will be of increased intensity. The reverse is also true, so silence and stillness equal low intensity. It is an excellent way to invite the audience to think.

Voice projection

Voice projection is the strength of speaking or singing through which your voice is used loudly and clearly. It is a technique which can be used to demand respect and attention, such as when a teacher is talking to the class, or simply to be heard clearly, as an actor in a theatre.

The breathe technique is great for proper voice projection. While on the other hand in normal <u>talking</u> one may use air from the top of the lungs, a properly projected voice uses air properly flowing from the expansion of the diaphragm. In good vocal technique, well-balanced breathing is especially important to maintaining vocal projection.

Using your voice

In the hours before your performance:

Do not rest your voice. Make sure that you have opportunities to talk. Talk to friends face to face or on the telephone. This will ensure that your voice does not become tense.

Find some opportunities to really stretch your articulators--your lips, your tongue, and your jaw. Singing is a good way to do this; so are reciting your own poems. Use your voice energetically, but without shouting.

As you begin to speak:

Stand up straight. This does not mean adopting an exaggerated stance, as though you were a soldier. Just lift your body and your head up and look forward in order to avoid a bent posture. It will help you to get into the correct posture if you imagine that you are balancing an object on your head. Remember, a bent or stiff posture will restrict your lung capacity.

Projecting your voice

By standing upright, you will maximize your vocal potential. By focusing on the need to be heard at the back of the room, you will project so that the sound echoes effortlessly throughout the whole space. This will also encourage you to open your mouth fully and articulate each sound. Speak a little slower than normal to begin with. Imagine that the person farthest from you is a little hard of hearing.

Be advised that your audience members begin to form an impression about you even before you open your mouth to speak. This view is based on what you look like and how you conduct yourself. The first impression they have of you shapes the way they are likely to initially respond to your piece.

The people you are talking to want you to look in control of yourself and the situation, confident in your manner, and pleased to be there.

It's not necessary to start speaking as soon as you see the whites of your audience's eyes. Take your time which is rare that you may have any during an event or show. If you do get a chance use the first few seconds to persuade the audience to like and trust you simply by how you are behaving. They will then be ready to listen appreciatively to your message.

Making the most out of your voice

Some public speakers feel their voice is not up to the job. This is not true. If you can hold an ordinary conversation, you can project successfully to an audience. It's as simple as that.

Your voice is an important instrument, and the anxiety of a performance that's about to happen can place a strain on it. Nor should you overcompensate by talking too loudly either.

To make the most of your voice, you only need to do two things. Before your performance, take measures to relax your voice. Then, during your performance, project correctly.

Relaxing your voice

Some speakers try to "save" their voice by talking as little as possible in the hours before their performance. This is a bad idea. To relax your voice before a performance, loosen your throat by exercising your voice by talking, practicing your poem or, especially, singing. You should also loosen your face muscles by stretching your lips and tongue and jaw—the body parts you use to articulate. Also, stand straight to encourage good vocal delivery, and talk, at a volume and intensity that does not cause strain, to the back of the room.

Movement and gesture

Body language may provide clues as to the attitude or state of mind of a person. For example, it may indicate aggression, attentiveness, boredom, relaxed state, pleasure, amusement, and intoxication, among many other cues.

Stance is also important, and it is recommended to stand up straight with your feet shoulder width apart and your upstage foot (right foot if right-handed etc.) slightly forward. This improves your balance and your breathing.

If a venue is so large or has such bad acoustics that you can't project properly without shouting, then use a microphone. If the audience members are too distant or you're outside, either move closer to them or ask people at the back to move closer.

To ensure you are heard, you also have to give yourself time to sufficiently articulate each consonant and vowel so that you can be heard without effort. This requires you to slow your speech down.

Remember, your voice will enhance your image as an excellent speaker provided you do the simple things required to relax and project it correctly.

The key element of a good speaker is being natural. Although a speaker may be speaking to dozens or even hundreds of people, he should be himself.

Movements and gestures look natural when they:

Have a purpose—you may make a lot of small gestures, with an occasional large gesture to emphasize a point. Adopt a basic standing position, which you can move from and then back to as you are speaking. Move closer to the audience when you want to achieve a greater intimacy.

Are not over controlled—don't stand in the same spot all the time and hide your hands behind your back. Don't retreat to the back of the room as though you are trying to hide from the audience.

Understanding body language

Your body is constantly speaking to your audience —whether you're conscious of it or not. Understanding how to read and use body language is essential to effective performances.

Using body language

Body language is sent and received from four different areas of body communication: facial expressions and eyes; hands and arms; body position and posture; and feet and legs. The messages can be subtle or quite noticeable, regardless of your intention.

Reinforcing Verbal Statements

Understanding body language signals is the first step in using this silent communication tool. Once you understand the signals, you can start using your body language to communicate more effectively. The next step is to reinforce your verbal statements by using body language to demonstrate complete communication, send messages, and emphasize key points.

Making a positive first impression

Your audience members begin to form an impression about you even before you open your mouth to speak. This view is based on what you look like and how you conduct yourself. The first impression they have of you shapes the way they are likely to respond to your piece, so you need to do all you can to make sure their impression of you is a good one.

Looking in control

The people you are talking to want you to look in control of yourself and the situation, confident in your manner, and pleased to be there.

Once your audience knows you are in control, they will begin to relax and listen to you.

Adopting a confident manner

Show you are confident in your ability by making good, strong eye contact with each person in the audience. Or you can do what is called an X scan, where you start with the upper right corner of the audience and slowly scan the crowd diagonally from that point. Once this is done you would go the upper left corner and repeat the same vision path, never really actually focusing on one person in the audience.

It's not necessary to start speaking as soon as you see the whites of your audience's eyes. If you get the chance take your time. Use the first few seconds to persuade the audience to like and trust you simply by how you are behaving. They will then be ready to listen appreciatively to your message.

A strong start

The first few minutes of your piece are critical. A strong start means capturing and holding the attention of your audience. Get the people in your audience interested from the start, and they are likely to stay with you. Lose them now, and you've probably lost them for good.

To capture the interest of your audience members from the very beginning, you must:

"Hook" the audience—Make a remark that will intrigue and interest the audience members and act as a "hook" for their attention so that they want to hear more. Using a startling fact or figure is a great way to make people sit up and take notice. Opening with a short, relevant personal account of an incident or event has the same effect.

Your opening remarks should provide a strong platform on which you can develop the rest of your piece. The first moments of your performance are crucial, so work hard to capture and hold your audience's attention.

Relating to your audience

One of the "wow factors" that makes a performance special is the speaker, simply through the language that he or she uses, encouraging and developing a relationship with the audience.

The techniques you need to establish personal interaction are the same for all audiences, although you may need to work a little harder with a large audience. Don't take up too much time doing so but to build a relationship with an audience, you should:
Allow your audience to get to know you—Do this by revealing information about yourself in the course of the performance either before or in between pieces and by revealing your own personal views

or feelings from time to time.

If you know your audience well already, interaction is usually easier. If you have not already met the people you will be speaking to, you need to find out more about them at the preparation stage. Always know your audience.

Making a great performance involves more than communicating in a dynamic and interesting way. You are in a room with other human beings. Make your presentation memorable by relating to them on a human level.

Keeping audience attention

Never make the mistake of assuming that because the audience members are initially interested in what you are saying, they will keep paying attention. If your performance lacks a clear development, you will lose the audience.

Your performance should be organized around its main points; they are the essential elements of the story you are telling. When these points and the connections between them are powerfully communicated to your audience, they command attention. Your story will have a clear development and be easy to follow.

As a speaker, you have to encourage and enable the audience to retain high concentration throughout by developing the content of your performance with crystal clarity. You can do this by strongly emphasizing: the end of each key point, the start of each new point, and the connection between points. You can use the following signals to signpost the main points of your talk.

Silence—Use silence to signal the end of a point; a silence of up to five seconds is acceptable. Look away from your audience at the same time to emphasize the break between the points.

Language—Use specific words and phrases as a way of signaling the end of one section, the start of another, or to indicate the connection between them.

Tempo—when you suddenly start to speak more slowly or more rapidly than normal, the audience will notice. You can use markedly rapid or slow speech to signal the end of one section or the start of a new one.

Using a combination of deliberate signals at key turning points ensures that your listeners always know what is important and are never lost.

As a speaker, you have to deal with the realities of your situation. The people in your audience have other things going on in their lives to distract them from your performance. To keep them concentrating, you have to signal the parts of the story as clearly as possible. Or to put it another way: Be listener-friendly!

A strong ending

The final impression that you leave in your audience members' minds will remain the longest. That's why the ending of your performance is so important.

By the time you approach the end of your performance, your audience has become accustomed to your voice and delivery and no matter how well you are doing, and it is harder to keep people concentrating on you than it was at the start. A strong ending means regaining audience attention by focusing attention on you, as the performer, and concentrating attention on your message.

The first thing you need to do is make the audience sit up and take notice by changing your style of delivery. The following techniques can help you do this:

Controlling your movement
Move around less than usual or stand in one place. This will concentrate attention on you. At the same time, link any noticeable gestures to your

words.

Controlling your voice
Make your audience concentrate by speaking more emphatically, stressing each important word and phrase.

Ending on a positive note
Usually, you do not want the people in your audience to be passive receivers of your message. Ending on a positive note is a tool that encourages people to translate the message into action. For example, predict success or tell the audience members how you want them to translate the message of your performance or story into action.

A strong ending is the best weapon you have in your armory to ensure the long-term success of your performance. It will help you to ensure that your audience members remember and act on what you have told them.

About the author

Darrell Mitchell II is a published author, poet, and artist. Since 1999 he has written and performed as a Spoken Word Artist known as D-Mitch the Poet and has also produced three spoken word albums, written, and published 20 Books, and created over 200 paintings and hosted numerous painting workshops. The artist was awarded the griot award by the San Fernando Valley Museum and the State Senator. He currently has performance videos that have gone viral and are currently viewed numerous times a throughout the day on national and international channels and websites.

The author's story has been described as inspirational, powerful, and enlightening. Most importantly he represents a family-friendly brand, which address everyday aspects of life and offers a different perspective. Through his work the author has moved generations, influenced ideas, and empowered readers and listeners to enjoy life and achieve their dreams.

Darrell Mitchell endeavors to encourage a generation to think better, write better and live better in life. As an organization we promote thinking on a creative level and assist with various aspects of performing arts through fundraising events, showcases and community outreach programs. His goal is to inspire, empower and enlighten the world through art and literature. The Artist/Writers brand represents products that readers can easily relate to. The current catalog has built a solid foundation among readers and music enthusiast, who currently read and listen to inspirational, empowering, and enlightening material.

www.ingramcontent.com/pod-product-compliance
Ingram Content Group UK Ltd.
Pitfield, Milton Keynes, MK11 3LW, UK
UKHW052101191224
3776UKWH00015B/118